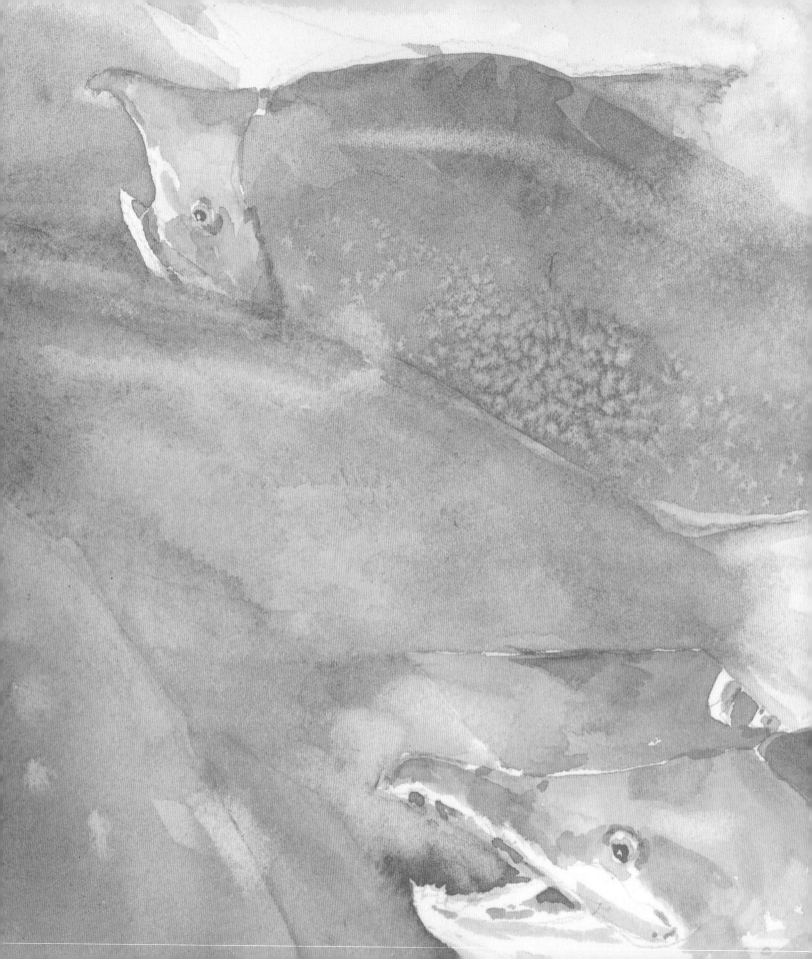

Salmon Forest

David Suzuki and Sarah Ellis
Illustrated by Sheena Lott

GREYSTONE BOOKS

Vancouver/Berkeley

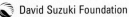

David Suzuki Foundation

It's a bright autumn day. Kate and her dad go to the river.

"Today we're going to find a story," says Dad. "It's called *The Salmon Forest*."

Kate skips along the trail and spots a chipmunk. "What's it about?"

"Mysteries, merry-go-rounds, and millions of babies," says Dad.

As they get close to the river, Kate smells something. "Yuck!"

Dead salmon lie in the shallows.

"Is that the end of the story already?" says Kate. "I don't want to go home yet."

"In this story, the beginning and the end are the same," says Dad. "That's one of the merry-go-rounds."

Kate and Dad hike farther up the river.

"What happened to those fish?"

"They came back from the ocean and swam way upstream to lay their eggs. Then they died and drifted downstream."

Kate peers into the river and sees a crowd of fish pushing and jostling against each other.

"Hey, look! The big red one jumped right out of the water!"

"That big guy is a male sockeye salmon," says Dad.

"Okay, I get it," says Kate. "The story is called The Salmon Forest because we're in the forest and there are the salmon."

"Yes, but there's more to it than that," says Dad. "It's also about the millions of babies and how the salmon and the forest need each other. These fish are on their way to a part of the river where there's a gravelly bottom and smooth-flowing water. That's where they can lay their eggs."

"I know about that," says Kate. "It's called the spawning area."

Dad stops. "Where did you find that out?"

"Video at school. We saw how the female makes a nest in the gravel with her tail and lays her eggs in it. But, Dad, you said the salmon need the forest. Why?"

"You'll see. Let's go closer to the river," says Dad.

Kate and Dad crouch by the river.

"Feel the water," says Dad.

"Brrr. It's cold!"

"Yes," says Dad. "That's good for the salmon eggs. They need cool water. Know what keeps it cool?"

Kate looks up into the trees. "Shade?"

"That's it. The forest is like a hat for the river, blocking the sun and keeping the river cool. That's one reason salmon need the forest."

"What's another reason?"

"The roots of the trees hold the soil in place so that it doesn't wash into the water and make it dirty. The eggs need clean water, and so do the baby salmon after they hatch."

"What happens next?" says Kate.

"After one or two summers, the salmon swim downstream. Most kinds of salmon go right to the ocean. But sockeye salmon find a lake and stay there for a year. Then they swim out to the sea."

"That's a long journey. Why do they go way out there?"

"Good question," says Dad. "When the eggs hatch, there are millions of baby fish in the stream but not enough food in the rivers and lakes to feed them. In the ocean there's lots of food, like needlefish and herring and oolichan. The salmon spend several years in the ocean, where they eat lots of fish. And seals, whales, and birds try to eat the salmon."

Kate and Dad climb a boulder.

"How do the salmon know when to come back to the river?"

"That's one of the mysteries," says Dad. "Somehow they know when it's time to make the long trip. They come back to lay their eggs."

"How do they find their way?"

"Mystery number two. They swim hundreds of kilometers out in the ocean, but they come right back to the river where they were born. Scientists think that every river has its own smell, which the fish recognize."

"Look," says Kate. "There's another red fish. I thought salmon were silver."

"The sockeye turn red as they move up the river," says Dad.

Kate looks up into the trees in their fall colors. "Then they match the leaves," she says.

Dad laughs. "Yes, they do."

Kate notices more dead salmon in the water.

"They make me feel sad," she says.

"Here's something to think about," says Dad. "All the fish want to do is reach their stream and spawn. They stop eating when they leave the ocean. They use all their energy to fight upstream, and they still have a long way to go from here. After they get to the gravel beds, they clean out a nest, lay their eggs, and then die. It's their natural life cycle. And the end of the story becomes the beginning."

"Because the eggs become baby salmon?" says Kate.

"Yes," says Dad. "And then an amazing thing happens."

"After a fish dies, its body is eaten by tiny bacteria and fungi, which are then eaten by insects. When the baby salmon hatch, they eat those bacteria and insects, which have been fed by their parents' bodies. So by dying, the parents have helped feed their babies."

"Bugs eat salmon. Salmon eat bugs. Another merry-go-round!" says Kate.

Gulls squawk overhead, and big black ravens hop along the riverbank.

"Birds are part of this story too," says Dad. "Flies lay eggs on the dead salmon, and the eggs hatch as maggots. The maggots eat the salmon flesh. Then, when the maggots grow into adult flies, songbirds eat them. So by feeding the maggots, the salmon also feed the birds."

Kate dances along the trail, playing hopscotch around fat green slugs. She makes up a song. "Bugs eat salmon, birds eat bugs. I eat macaroni, but I don't eat slugs."

Suddenly Kate sees a bear walk onto a rock where the river narrows.

"Is it dangerous?" she whispers.

"No, we're a long way from it. Besides, it's only interested in eating the salmon, its favorite food."

The bear plunges its head into the water and comes up with a fish, which struggles to escape.

Kate and Dad watch the bear carry the salmon away.

"Bears like to eat alone," says Dad. "That bear will take its fish into the forest and eat the yummiest parts, like the brain and belly. Then it will probably leave the rest of the fish and come back to catch more. As the fish rots, the nutrients from its body go into the soil. In that way, the salmon fertilizes the forest."

"There's some bear poop!" says Kate.

"Good spotting," says Dad. "More fertilizer for the forest."

"So that's why the forest needs the salmon."

"Right. All the poop from the bears, eagles, otters, ravens, coyotes, and other animals that eat salmon helps the forest grow."

"And the forest grows and shades the salmon spawning grounds," says Kate.

"And the salmon feed the animals," says Dad.

Kate laughs. "And the animals feed the forest. That's another merry-go-round."

"And who's on all the merry-go-rounds?"

"Salmon!" says Kate. She spins around. "Salmon river, salmon eagle, salmon poop, salmon trees, salmon forest."

Farther on, Kate and Dad see a man and a boy standing near a big boulder by the river. The man is holding a long pole with a hook on one end. He puts that end into the water and suddenly jerks it to snag a salmon. The boy grabs the struggling fish and kills it by hitting it on the head with a club.

"What do you know?" says Dad. "There's Simon, with Brett."

"Hi, Brett!" Kate yells.

The boy grins and waves them over.

"How's the fishing?" says Dad.

"Great," says Brett. "We've just started and have already caught three nice salmon. Mom and Patricia are over there cleaning them." He points to a table under a tarp not far away.

"You mean they're giving them a bath?" says Kate with a giggle.

"No, silly," says Brett. "Go have a look."

"Edna," says Dad, "good to see you again. And how are you, Patricia?"

Kate watches Edna and Patricia take the guts out of the salmon and remove the head and backbone from the fish. They cut out the ribs, then make a series of deep slices in the meat. Edna's hands are flying.

"You sure are fast," says Kate.

"I learned by watching my granny when I was a girl," says Edna.

"What do you do with the fish when they're clean?" says Kate.

"Some of them will be prepared for smoking, others will be sliced so they can dry out in the wind, and others will be frozen or bottled. And of course, we'll cook some of them fresh," says Edna.

"We're cooking some right now," says Brett. "My favorite way. Baked with soy sauce, sugar, and garlic."

"Yesterday fried was your favorite way," says Patricia.

"Whatever way we cook it is Brett's favorite way," laughs Edna. "He's a real salmon boy. Which makes sense, because we call ourselves fish people. We couldn't survive without salmon."

"Just like salmon babies and animals and trees," says Kate. "Seems like everybody needs salmon."

Edna nods. "Our people say, 'In nature, everything is connected.'"

"Hey, we forgot about Dad!" says Patricia. "Brett, tell him to come and take a break."

"Why don't you stay and have tea and baked salmon with us?" Edna says to Kate and Dad.

"Can we, can we?" says Kate.

"Sure," says Dad. "That would be great."

Brett and Simon return with more fish. Patricia fills cups with tea and lots of milk and sugar, and Edna gives everyone a piece of fish.

"Mmm, that's so good," says Kate. "Daddy? When we eat salmon we're like the bears and bugs and trees, right? It's like we're salmon humans."

Dad grins. "You've got it, Kate. We're all part of the same story."

Brett's Favorite Salmon

One of Brett's favorite ways to cook salmon is barbecued with a sweet teriyaki sauce. The best part is catching the salmon first. If you buy the fish at a market, try to get a wild salmon.

You will need:

60 mL (¼ cup)	sugar
125 mL (½ cup)	soy sauce
2	large cloves garlic, peeled and chopped
5-cm (2-inch)	piece of ginger root
1-kg (2-pound)	fillet of salmon
	parsley

Stir the sugar into the soy sauce. (You can heat the mixture in a microwave oven for 15 seconds to dissolve the sugar.) Add the garlic. Grate the ginger into the sauce. Taste it—mmm, yummy!

Cut the salmon into four pieces. Dunk each piece into the sauce and make sure that it is well coated. Place the salmon on a grill heated to 175°C (350°F). Spoon some of the sauce on top of the fish.

Grill until you see the fish change color through about a quarter of the thickness of the pieces. Then flip them over. Spoon some of the sauce on the top sides (now cooked). Cook and remove the salmon when just the center is still red.

Serve decorated with a sprig of parsley. When you put a piece in your mouth, you will know why salmon is one of the world's best fish for eating.

Serves 4

Glossary

Bacteria Creatures so small that you can only see them with a microscope; often called germs.

Fertilize To make soil richer so that plants can grow better in it.

Fungi A group of organisms such as mushrooms, yeast, and mold. They are similar to plants but reproduce by means of spores rather than seeds.

Maggot The legless, wormlike stage of a fly, just after it leaves the egg.

Nutrient A substance in food that is necessary for life.

Spawning area The place where fish deposit their eggs.

18 19 20 21 22   13 12 11 10 9

Greystone Books Ltd.
www.greystonebooks.com

David Suzuki Foundation
219-2211 West 4th Avenue
Vancouver, British Columbia v6k 4s2

Cataloguing data available from Library and Archives Canada

ISBN 978-1-55365-163-5 (PBK.)
ISBN 978-1-92670-626-9 (EPDF)

Cover and text design by Gabi Proctor/DesignGeist
Printed and bound in China by 1010 Printing International Ltd.
Distributed in the U.S. by Publishers Group West

The authors gratefully acknowledge the assistance of Kit Pearson and Dr. Tom Reimchen.

We gratefully acknowledge the financial support of the Canada Council for the Arts,
the British Columbia Arts Council, the Province of British Columbia through the Book
Publishing Tax Credit, and the Government of Canada through the Canada Book Fund
for our publishing activities.

Greystone Books is committed to reducing the consumption of old-growth forests in
the books it publishes. This book is one step towards that goal.